Gandhi

Library of Congress Control Number: 2018936549
ISBN 978-1-250-30254-0

Our books may be purchased in bulk for promotional, educational, or business use. Please contact your local bookseller or the Macmillan Corporate and Premium Sales Department at (800) 221-7945 ext. 5442 or by e-mail at MacmillanSpecialMarkets@macmillan.com.

First published in France in 2017 by Quelle Histoire, Paris
First U.S. edition, 2018

Text: Clémentine V. Baron
Translation: Catherine Nolan
Illustrations: Bruno Wennagel, Mathieu Ferret, Aurélie Verdon, Nuno Alves Rodrigues, Guillaume Biasse, Mathilde Tuffin, Sophie D'Hénin

Printed in China by RR Donnelley Asia Printing Solutions Ltd., Dongguan City, Guangdong Province
10 9 8 7 6 5 4 3 2 1

Gandhi

Roaring Brook Press
New York

Childhood

Mohandas Karamchand Gandhi was born in India in 1869. He was an honest, well-behaved boy. He adored his mother and admired his father. When his father was sick, Gandhi took care of him.

Gandhi and his family belonged to the Hindu religion. Following Hindu tradition, Gandhi married very young. He and his bride were only thirteen years old!

———

1869–1882

Studying in London

In 1888, Gandhi went to England to study law. His mother was worried. She made him promise to respect the customs of Hinduism. He could not eat meat or drink wine.

Gandhi obeyed. But he began to dress like an Englishman, in suits and ties. Sometimes he even wore a top hat and carried a fancy cane!

Later in life, Gandhi would dress very differently, wearing a simple cloth wrapped around his body.

——

1888–1891

Two Colonies

After three years, Gandhi returned to India with his law degree. He had a good education, but he was too shy to find any clients.

Finally, Gandhi found a job in South Africa and moved there with his family. One day, Gandhi tried to ride in the first-class car of a train in South Africa. He was told he could not because he was Indian. Then he was thrown off the train!

At this time, India and South Africa were both colonies of Great Britain. They were ruled by white colonists who treated everyone else poorly. It was unfair and racist.

1891–1893

South Africa

Gandhi decided to fight for Indians' rights in South Africa. But he did not fight with his fists. Instead, he used his head.

Over many years, Gandhi did everything he could to improve life for Indians. He negotiated with generals, organized marches, and was even arrested for defending his beliefs! The protests worked: Some of the harsh measures against Indians were finally dropped in 1914.

For the first time, Gandhi and his fellow protestors had used nonviolent movements to make change. This way of "fighting with peace" was called *satyagraha*.

———

1893–1914

Exploring India

In 1914, Gandhi decided to use satyagraha in his home country.

He went back and spent a year traveling around India. He met artists and great thinkers who helped him shape his ideas. He also started an *ashram*—a place where he and others could go to meditate.

Now Gandhi was ready to fight peacefully for justice in India. He began by defending the rights of peasants and workers. People were grateful. They called him "Bapu," which means "father," and "Mahatma," which means "great soul."

—

1914–1916

Politics

Gandhi didn't like politics, but he knew it was a powerful way to change society. He eventually became the leader of the Indian National Congress party. He worked hard to help the poor, women, and other groups that faced discrimination.

Gandhi often used "political fasting" to make his voice heard. He would starve himself until his demands were met! Gandhi went on hunger strikes many times in his life, often coming close to death.

——

1917–1948

The Amritsar Massacre

Many Indians, including Gandhi, felt that their country should be independent—that India should no longer be a British colony. On April 13, 1919, a peaceful rally against British rule was held in Amritsar, a holy city in India.

The British Army fired on the crowd, killing almost four hundred people. Gandhi was outraged. In protest, he told Indians to take action against the British government, like not buying any British products.

Gandhi's protest was nonviolent, but riots broke out across India, and the British government blamed Gandhi. In 1922, he went to prison for two years.

———

1919–1922

The Salt March

Gandhi organized another protest in 1930. The British had a tax on salt in India. Gandhi declared that he would walk to the sea and "steal" a handful of salt without paying the tax.

Thousands of people left their jobs to join Gandhi on his 241-mile march. Many of them were arrested, including Gandhi himself.

———

1930

Quit India

Twelve years later, India was still fighting for independence. Gandhi started a movement called Quit India. He demanded that British people who lived in India leave the country for good.

Gandhi was arrested again, and the movement failed. But it made Great Britain realize that India was never going to stop fighting. British leaders began to talk with Indian leaders about finding a path to freedom.

———

1942

The Final Struggle

India finally won its independence in 1947! Gandhi should have been overjoyed, but he wasn't. This new India was not a united country; it was split in two over religious differences. There was a Hindu side, which kept the name India, and a Muslim side, called Pakistan.

Gandhi wanted the two sides to come together and make one nation. He urged his fellow Hindus to show more tolerance toward Muslims, but some would not. One man grew so angry at the suggestion that he shot and killed Gandhi in January 1948.

Long after his death, Gandhi's peaceful protests inspired other great leaders, like Martin Luther King Jr. and Nelson Mandela. He is still a role model to many all over the world.

———

1947–1948

1865

1869
Gandhi is born in Porbandar on October 2.

1888
Gandhi goes to London to study law.

1893
Gandhi takes a job in South Africa.

1882
Gandhi marries Kasturbai.

1891
Gandhi returns to India after passing his bar exam.

1917-1918
Gandhi fights for peasants in Bihar and mill workers in Ahmedabad.

1922
Gandhi is sentenced to six years in prison but is released after two.

1930
Gandhi launches the 241-mile Salt March.

1944
Kasturbai dies in prison.

1948
Gandhi is assassinated on January 30 in New Delhi.

1950

1914
Thanks in part to Gandhi's efforts, an agreement is signed to improve life for Indians in South Africa.

1919
The Amritsar massacre takes place.

1924
Gandhi holds a twenty-one-day hunger strike for peace between Hindus and Muslims.

1942
Gandhi works on the Quit India movement.

1947
India's independence is proclaimed.

Gandhi's Journey

1 Porbandar, India

Gandhi was born in this small coastal town. It's nicknamed the "white city" because many of its houses are made of pale stone.

2 London, England

Gandhi went to law school in this British city for three years.

3 Durban, South Africa

Like India, South Africa was a British colony. Gandhi led his first campaign against racial injustice in the city of Durban.

4 Amritsar, India

Nearly four hundred Indians were killed by the British Army during a peaceful demonstration here in 1919.

5 Dandi, India

In 1930, Gandhi made a 241-mile march to the coastal town of Dandi to protest a salt tax. Thousands of Indians joined him.

6 New Delhi, India

Gandhi spent the last months of his life in the capital of India. He was assassinated here on January 30, 1948.

People to Know

Kasturbai (or Kasturba) Gandhi
(1869–1944)
She married Mohandas Gandhi at the age of thirteen and had four sons with him. Indians thought of her as the mother of their country and affectionately nicknamed her "Ma."

Jawaharlal Nehru
(1889–1964)
Jawaharlal was one of Gandhi's main supporters. He even followed Gandhi to prison! In 1947, he became the first prime minister of India.

Lord Louis Mountbatten
(1900–1979)
Louis, a British earl, was named viceroy of India
in 1947. He was the last person to hold the title
before India won its independence.

Martin Luther King Jr.
(1929–1968)
This African American pastor is one of the
most famous figures of the American civil
rights movement. Inspired by Gandhi, Martin
preached equality and organized peaceful
demonstrations. He was only thirty-nine
years old when he was assassinated.

....

Gandhi ate only fruit, nuts, and seeds for five years. He had to change to a fully vegetarian diet because of health issues.

....

Gandhi traveled around with a goat named Nirmala to ensure that he always had fresh goat's milk to drink.

....

More than two million people attended Gandhi's funeral. The funeral procession was almost five miles long.

....

Gandhi thought soccer was a noble sport. He started three soccer clubs during his time in South Africa.

Available Now

Muhammad Ali

Neil Armstrong

Blackbeard

Coco Chanel

Charlie Chaplin

Cleopatra

Marie Curie

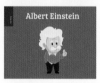
Albert Einstein

Anne Frank

Gandhi

Frida Kahlo

Martin Luther King Jr.

Abraham Lincoln

Nelson Mandela

Isaac Newton

Rosa Parks

Coming Soon

Marie Antoinette

Buddha

Pocahontas

Vincent van Gogh